DK ESSE ... GERS

Gr...

Business

BIBI VAN DER ZEE

London, New York,
Munich, Melbourne, Delhi

Senior Editor Peter Jones
Senior Art Editor Helen Spencer
Executive Managing Editor Adèle Hayward
Managing Art Editor Kat Mead
Art Director Peter Luff
Publisher Stephanie Jackson
Production Editor Ben Marcus
Production Controller Hema Gohil

Produced for Dorling Kindersley Limited by

cobaltid

The Stables, Wood Farm, Deopham Road,
Attleborough, Norfolk NR17 1AJ
www.cobaltid.co.uk

Editors Louise Abbott, Kati Dye,
Maddy King, Marek Walisiewicz
Designers Darren Bland, Claire Dale,
Paul Reid, Annika Skoog, Lloyd Tilbury

First published in 2008 by
Dorling Kindersley Limited
80 Strand
London WC2R 0RL
A Penguin Company

A CIP catalogue record for this book
is available from the British Library.

ISBN 978-1-4053-3155-5

Colour reproduction by
Colourscan, Singapore
Printed in China by WKT

See our complete catalogue at

www.dk.com

Contents

Introduction

With daily stories of record temperatures, extreme weather, and floods and droughts, and of renewable energy, carbon footprints, recycling, and energy efficiency, the environment is increasingly becoming headline news. The world's governments are moving slowly towards new international agreements that will start to address the impact of business on the environment, and these, undoubtedly, will place new requirements on every organization.

But the situation is too urgent to wait for governments alone to act, and today's consumers expect every business to take responsibility for its actions – to look at the way it operates and measure its environmental impact, and then put in place a strategy to reduce it. Furthermore, businesses will have to become expert in communicating these changes to their customers.

This book will help you make tough decisions, giving you a raft of options, suggestions, and concrete advice on how to go green. It includes case studies to show you how other businesses have done it, arguments to help persuade your own organization into action, and advice on how to take your green message to your consumers. Every person and business can make a difference, but work needs to start right away.

Chapter 1

The environment and the business world

It is increasingly becoming clear that our planet is under growing environmental stress. Green issues raise serious concerns and present challenges that can no longer be ignored by the business world.

The case for going green

Business has traditionally assumed that "going green" – incorporating environmental issues into business strategy – costs money. It is becoming clear, however, that not taking care of the environment will bring costs of its own, and that businesses that fail to go green will pay in the future.

Why go green?

Going green is no longer seen as an expensive indulgence that will not improve a business's bottom line, or as window-dressing that will not make any difference to the planet in the long-term. Decision-makers are increasingly rejecting the idea that there is no opportunity or growth potential for a truly green company. Despite the economic turbulence of the early 21st century, one thing has become clear: today's industry leaders include organizations that have embraced radical environmental policies, and have profited from them.

Leading the way

When international trade conditions are challenging and insecurity about the future widespread, going green may seem a particularly daunting move. But some of today's most successful organizations have made the decision to reshape themselves from the bottom up, improving their environmental profile and their public image, making financial savings and safeguarding against future environmental hazards. Businesses such as Pelamis – which produces energy from wave power – and Toyota, whose research and development of hybrid motors has made it the industry leaders in green automobiles, are forging ahead in green technologies, highlighting the sorts of opportunity that will open up in the future.

Staying ahead

Around the world, environmental regulations are being put into place, or tightened, and it is increasingly likely that in the future, firms that continue to have an adverse impact on the environment will be heavily fined or restricted. There is also a growing demand for corporate reporting, which will mean that organizations will find it harder and harder to cover up any unethical or environmentally unfriendly practices. And just as investors can be scared off a company with a poor history of health and safety, so the stock market value of non-green businesses could also be affected. Those that have already cleaned up their act are likely to have the best chance of staying ahead of the game.

IN FOCUS... THE HARD-HEADED REASONS FOR GOING GREEN

Recognizing the value of adopting green strategies will have visible positive impacts on your efficiency and profitability:

- Not having environmental credentials precludes you from tendering for many contracts – especially large governmental contracts.
- A study of UK graduates showed that almost half would refuse to take up job offers from businesses they considered unethical.
- Green practices, such as encouraging homeworking, have been shown to boost staff productivity by up to one-fifth.
- Adopting environmentally sustainable practices can directly cut your costs and increase your profits.

CASE STUDY

Green returns

After 20 years of cutting down its emissions of the gases responsible for climate change, the US science and technology company DuPont, which had revenues of $27.3bn in 2004, estimates that it has saved $3bn. Its technological innovators first began assessing its emissions in 1991, and went on to invest $50m to retrofit some of its facilities to reduce emissions, by up to 55 per cent in some cases. It has reduced its energy use by 9 per cent while continuing to grow. This forward-thinking approach has meant that DuPont is now right at the forefront of a market that is beginning to respond to climate change, and provides a blueprint for many businesses that want to go green.

Consumer pressure

One of the most compelling arguments for a business to go green comes from customers. Surveys of consumer attitudes to sustainability and the environment show a consistent and steady growth in the demand for responsible products and green working practices; in one survey, more than 25 per cent of consumers stated that they would not buy from organizations that have a poor environmental track record. Businesses that convince customers that the money they spend will not be used to damage the planet will find that consumers respond well.

Making the environmental case

The backdrop for these changing attitudes to green business is one of rapid environmental change. Industrialization is putting the earth under increasing stress. Cities are sprawling out into the country, and the world's wildlife is under threat as its habitats are destroyed. Industrial pollution is damaging ecosystems in oceans and rivers, and air pollution is choking urban areas. Increasing amounts of waste are being dumped in overflowing landfill sites. Natural resources are rapidly vanishing, rainforests are being lost, and the oil used to drive our modern lifestyles is in shorter supply. It is clear that these environmental issues raise concerns that must be addressed by industries and businesses.

The greatest environmental challenge we are facing, however, is climate change. In 2007, the Intergovernmental Panel on Climate Change (IPCC) – an international scientific body convened by the United Nations (UN) – produced its fourth assessment report on climate change. This stated unequivocally that the earth's atmosphere is warming, and that the warming is very likely to be the result of human activity.

The panel also looked to the future, and predicted that if we do not respond, climate change is likely to imperil food supplies, wipe out whole animal and plant species, and cause floods and epidemics of disease. The IPCC's conclusion is that if we do nothing, climate change will, in the long term, be likely to "exceed the capacity of natural, managed, and human systems to adapt."

IN FOCUS... THE TRIPLE BOTTOM LINE

People, planet, and profits are the three factors that make up the triple bottom line. This concept asks that organizations don't just take the financial capital involved in business into account, but also the human capital – the well-being of all individuals, be they workers or the local community – and the natural capital. This term refers to our environmental resources. As these start to become scarce, it will become increasingly difficult to treat the natural world as a freely available, infinitely renewable resource. The triple bottom line recognizes this reality, and compels businesses to conserve, not waste, resources.

Understanding climate change

Before the industrial revolution, changes to the earth's environment in history were natural – part of the cycle of life. Modern lifestyles, however, are now causing serious damage, and if working habits do not change soon, we run the risk of making the earth uninhabitable.

The changing climate

*Greenhouse gas — *any gas that, once in the atmosphere, contributes to the warming of the earth.*

*Carbon dioxide — *a gas at standard temperatures and pressures; it is often referred to simply as "carbon".*

*Anthropogenic — *resulting from human activities.*

Over the past century, the climate of the earth has steadily warmed, the average surface temperature increasing by about 0.75°C. The earth's climate has always varied naturally, bringing warmer and colder periods – such as the ice ages – but scientists now think that the recent warming of the climate is the result of human activity. The problem lies with the greenhouse gases* (GHGs) that we are producing in increasing quantities – particularly carbon dioxide* (CO_2), but also nitrous oxide (N_2O), methane (CH_4), and a group of gases known as halocarbons. The global rise in temperature over the last 100 years correlates closely with the increased anthropogenic* production of these GHGs.

The greenhouse effect

Accumulation of GHGs in the atmosphere is believed to be contributing to a process known as the greenhouse effect. Energy that hits the earth from the sun is absorbed by the earth's surface, which radiates it back. GHGs in the atmosphere prevent this heat energy from escaping into space, instead radiating it back to earth and causing the climate to warm. As the amount of GHG emissions increases, so the climate warms further.

IN FOCUS... GREENHOUSE GASES

- Carbon dioxide (CO_2) can be produced by the combustion of fossil fuels, such as oil and coal, to generate electricity and power vehicles, and also in the production of cement for construction.
- Methane (CH_4) is produced during the decomposition of organic matter, such as in landfills. Agriculture, and in particular the gaseous emissions of livestock animals, is also a major source of this GHG.

- Nitrous oxide (N_2O) is produced naturally by bacteria in the oceans and in soils, but anthropogenic N_2O emissions have increased through the use of nitrogen fertilizers, and the production of animal waste.
- Halocarbons, such as the chlorofluorocarbons (CFCs) contribute to the greenhouse effect. They were used in aerosol sprays until legislation in the late 1980s controlled their use.

Increasing emissions

The major sources of anthropogenic GHGs are (in descending order): energy production, industry, forestry, agriculture, and transport. All businesses produce GHG emissions through the electricity they use to power their operations; through the manufacturing process used to make their products; from the resources and raw materials needed; the waste generated and sent to landfill; and from the transport costs for shipping and distribution.

Of the GHGs, CO_2 is the greatest contributor to climate change. Annual emissions of CO_2 increased by about 80 per cent between 1970 and 2004, and levels of CO_2 in the atmosphere are now higher than they have been for 650,000 years.

Global impacts

The effects of climate change will vary considerably around the planet, and countries will find that they are facing their own challenges. The warming of the oceans and melting ice at the poles is contributing to sea-level rise, increasing the risk of flooding in low-lying areas. This threatens a number of major cities, including Hong Kong, London, New York, Shanghai, and Tokyo. Desertification threatens areas of Australia, Africa, and parts of the Far East, and predictions are that an increase in global temperature of 4°C would see a worldwide decline in major crop yields. Some areas have already seen an increase in extreme weather events – it is predicted that these will become more and more frequent as the climate warms.

Rising costs and responsibilities

Rising costs linked to climate change have huge implications for the business world. Insurers, for example, have realized the risk that climate change presents to them, and their models for prediction are increasingly being built to factor in the effects of climate change. Rising energy prices present a serious consideration for all businesses, as do increasing complications with waste disposal, while the growing amount of legislation being put in place to deal with climate change will impose a new set of responsibilities.

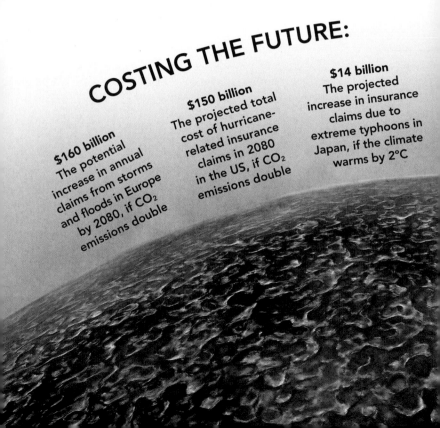

COSTING THE FUTURE:

$160 billion
The potential increase in annual claims from storms and floods in Europe by 2080, if CO_2 emissions double

$150 billion
The projected total cost of hurricane-related insurance claims in 2080 in the US, if CO_2 emissions double

$14 billion
The projected increase in insurance claims due to extreme typhoons in Japan, if the climate warms by 2°C

Mitigation and adaptation

In the face of the major changes climate change will bring to the world in which we do business, countries and organizations have two paths before them. Firstly, steps can be taken to fight the effects of climate change by reducing CO_2 emissions. This is known as mitigation, and will reduce the need for the second response to global warming: adaptation. As the environment changes, governments and businesses will have to be prepared to adapt to a set of new challenges, and also be ready to take any opportunites that arise.

QUANTIFYING THE IMPACTS:

200 million
Number of refugees that could be created by flooding and drought worldwide by 2050 if climate warms by 2–3°C

33 per cent
The predicted reduction in agricultural crop yields across the continent of Africa if the climate warms by 4°C

10.8 per cent
The amount China's GDP is predicted to be reduced by if there was a sea-level rise of 5m (16ft)

International action

The international community has come together to take action against the threat of climate change, and the implications of its decisions will have a major impact on the business world. At the same time, individual countries are starting to put in place measures to mitigate and adapt to localized effects of the changing climate.

Setting benchmarks

History shows that swift action and regulation can address many environmental problems. In Japan in the 1970s, for example, the government reacted decisively to the problems of toxic waste and air pollution from industry, creating the Environment Agency and putting rigorous restrictions in place: as a result, air pollution has declined while industrial growth has continued.

Responding to the threat of climate change has been firmly on the international agenda for more than two decades. At the 1992 Earth Summit in Rio de Janeiro, the UN produced The United Nations Framework Convention on Climate Change (UNFCCC or FCCC). In this ground-breaking environmental treaty, industrialized signatories agreed to reduce their emission levels to below 1990 levels. The Kyoto Protocol – a codicil to the UNFCCC – was signed in Japan in 1997, and commits most industrialized countries to reducing their emissions by six to eight per cent below 1990 levels by 2012. However, the US – one of the world's largest contributors of CO_2 emissions – has refused to ratify Kyoto and so is not bound by these targets.

In 2007, the Bali Roadmap was formulated at the Conference of the Parties (COP13) as a step towards reaching final agreement on the successor to Kyoto.

Global measures

The unique challenges faced by every country and the responses they choose will have major implications for firms based, or hoping to do business, there.

- In India, for example, rapid population growth is leading to increasing environmental problems. In response, it is now the world's fourth largest producer of wind power and is encouraging the development of other renewable energy sources.

- In Europe, the European Emission Trading Scheme (ETS) – the world's largest carbon trading scheme – has been set up. The Common Agricultural Policy that subsidizes farming has been amended to encourage more sustainable farming practices.

- In Brazil, the greatest challenge being faced is preventing the huge deforestation that is presenting a serious threat to the climate. International negotiators are working hard to find a way to include forest conservation in the legislation that will become the successor to the Kyoto agreement.

- In China, tackling the congestion and air pollution problem that plagues the populous country's cities is an urgent priority. The government has set itself the task of improving industrial recyling, water use, and energy efficiency, and is building eco cities that will ban cars from their centres and have the latest waste and energy technologies in place.

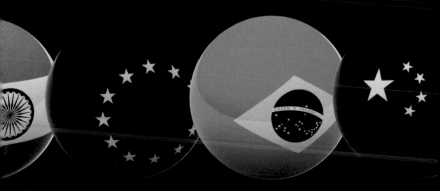

Chapter 2

Developing a green business strategy

Planning a long-term strategy for greening your business needs to be a thorough and careful process – you are embarking on a complex journey that will transform both the way that your business operates and the way that you think.

Going green

Some of the world's most successful organizations – from Wal-Mart to News Corporation – now perceive the environment as foremost amongst their responsibilities, and are making sweeping changes that incorporate green issues into the heart of their business strategies.

Leading the pack

Going green is still a profoundly untested field, and one in which there are few certainties. Many of the pioneering businesses that are attempting to reduce their impact on the environment and improve their sustainability are out there on their own, mapping uncharted territories. However, facing increasing legislation on environmental issues and growing consumer pressure, today's businesses are having to take seriously the call to go green. Organizations that heed this call will be best placed to lead their fields, while those that fail to do so will be left behind.

Committing yourself

As a green pioneer, you will find that you have to overcome many difficulties and change firmly held beliefs. Some of the ways that you have always worked will have to change. You may need to consider large financial outlays to purchase new equipment or fund restructuring, and have to convince staff, customers, and investors that going green is the right thing to do. You may make mistakes, even costly ones, that mean you have to backtrack and start again. So it is vital that you are completely committed to going green – you need to have an unshakable belief that this is the right direction to take if you are going to bring everyone else along with you. It's worth reminding yourself that what you are doing is not just about business, it's also about the future for your family, your friends, your planet: everything that is really important.

BE POSITIVE

Take an enthusiastic and open-minded approach to transforming your business, and be crystal clear about why you are doing it.

THINKING GREEN

FAST TRACK	OFF TRACK
Looking for potential and possibility	Trying to find reasons why you can't go green
Being prepared to honestly assess the activities of your company	Looking for ways that you can mask your problems rather than deal with them
Enthusing yourself and your staff about the greening process	Thinking you can rush ahead without making sure everyone is on board
Adopting a can-do attitude about tackling climate change	Making yourself and your staff feel anxious about the environment

Planning a green strategy

Sustainable business means thinking cyclically: using resources and energy conservatively, not assuming they are infinite, and considering the full life-cycle of your products, including what happens to them once they leave your hands and once their usefulness is over. And it means, most of all, continually working with an eye to the future.

TIP

CHALLENGE CONVENTIONAL THINKING

Be prepared to completely reassess the way you look at all aspects of your business, from the waste you produce and the energy you use, to the packaging you supply your products in and the suppliers that you get your resources from.

Thinking cyclically

Coming up with a green strategy for your business involves a radical rethink of how you work. Traditional approaches to business thinking have been strictly linear: design a product; manufacture the product; sell the product. But this makes no allowance for what happens to products once they are off the shelf, or for what happens to waste: resources such as water, fuel, and paper are often used with little thought given to environmental impact or recycling possibilities.

The current situation, with resources becoming more expensive and scarce, and the environment under threat, proves the traditional approach is unsustainable. Instead, business needs to be thinking cyclically, in a closed loop. Issues of sustainability need to be deeply incorporated into business strategies and planning techniques. Waste, for example, needs to be thought of as a potential resource, and raw materials need to be chosen because they come from sustainable sources, not just because of their price.

Start planning in a cyclical way. Don't just launch a green strategy and then rest on your laurels – continually refresh your thinking, return to your original impulse, and revisit the numbers. Think of the whole process as a cycle of improvement.

Devising your green strategy

1 LOOK AT THE BIG PICTURE
Assess your business as a whole: what does it do, who does it serve, where is it based, and where is it going?

2 FORMULATE YOUR VISION
Think about how you see the future of your business in the short and medium term.

3 ASSESS YOURSELF
Use a "green audit" to take a thorough look at your current practices, and where you could improve.

4 SET GOALS
Define specific targets to aim for and set dates for when you want to achieve them.

5 CHOOSE YOUR TACTICS
Look for ways, both innovative and straightforward, to achieve the goals you have set.

6 IMPLEMENT YOUR STRATEGY
Communicate your tactics to your staff and start to implement them, monitoring your progress.

7 COMMUNICATE THE CHANGES
Let your customers and shareholders know what you are doing and why you are doing it.

8 THINK CYCLICALLY
Constantly reassess and refresh your thinking by beginning the process once more.

HOW TO...
REACH
YOUR
GOALS

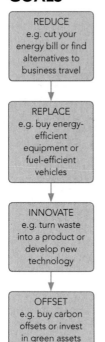

Setting goals

Strategic planning is all about setting out a long-term vision, identifying the goals you want to aim for, and then choosing the tactics required to get there. Larger businesses have their long-term strategies mapped out in great detail, but even the smallest business can benefit from this approach. However, businesses setting the goals of a green strategy face a problem: there is, at present, no best practice relating to environmental strategy and carbon reduction, only leading practice. You may find that this is also an advantage: establishing a reputation for your business as a ground-breaker is no bad thing.

When choosing goals, keep an open-minded approach. You may decide that you want to concentrate on improving those aspects of your business, such as CO_2 emissions, that would appeal most to your clients and customers. However, you could then miss out on other areas to make a significant difference to your environmental impact, such as rethinking your waste and resource management procedures. Achieving compliance – being sure that you are aware of and meeting international legal standards – will be an increasingly important area for all businesses to include in their green strategy.

Getting started

Effective implementation of your strategy is vital if it is to be successful. Once you have clearly defined your goals, and have devised a set of tactics to reach them, the next step is to communicate these goals clearly throughout your organization to make sure that everyone understands what has to be done and why. And once your strategy is in operation, you will need an effective monitoring system to keep track of your progress, and ensure that your tactics are working.

CHOOSING TACTICS

AREA	POTENTIAL GOALS	TACTICS
Overall sustainability of your organization	Produce a green business strategy and integrate it within 18 months.	Appoint a "green team" – members of staff dedicated to developing your green strategy and implementing it; develop and market a few products with excellent green credentials that you can use as a trailblazer for the rest of your business.
CO_2 emissions	Reduce total CO_2 emissions by 10 per cent per year, or achieve carbon neutrality by a specific target date.	Implement a range of carbon-cutting strategies, such as improved energy efficiency; shared transport for staff; or reduction of freight journeys.
Waste management	Reduce the amount of waste produced by your business by 30 per cent within the next two years; increase recycling; find an innovative way of reusing your waste.	Appoint a waste manager; initiate contact with waste researchers to find innovative ways to reduce or reuse the waste you produce; put a thorough recycling system in place throughout your operations.
Compliance	Achieve full compliance by year end.	Assign the duty of monitoring compliance to a member of staff; if changes are needed, instigate projects to achieve them.
Resource usage	Implement a green purchasing strategy; reduce water usage by 10 per cent within 10 months; reduce resource usage.	Use recycled materials where possible; replace existing machinery with more water-efficient models; build waste costs into your planning in order to encourage reduction at the planning level.
Green assets and new technologies	Identify four possible purchases within four months.	Assign the task of identifying acquisitions of green assets to a member of staff; discuss and identify ideal requirements and qualities.
Communication	Publish a Corporate Social Responsibility (CSR) report within six months; ally your firm with a green community project within six months.	Select a team to plan and write the CSR report; begin research into suitable community projects.

Getting everyone on board

If your green vision is to be successful, all members of staff must be committed to making it a reality. This is much more likely if you have convinced them of its benefits to your organization, and made them feel that they are going to play an important part in the process of going green.

Making the case

It is crucial to engage your staff right from the beginning, and to reassure them that implementing a green business strategy will be a positive experience. Let them know that you welcome their input, and if any of their ideas end up being incorporated into your green strategy, make sure that you give them credit. You may find that some of your staff feel anxious about the radical changes you are planning, so work hard to bring them along with you. Create a forum in which concerns about the process you are undertaking can be aired, and respond to any issues that are raised. It is also important to recognize achievements and reward successes, such as when you hit a target or win an award. This doesn't cost the business much but has a significant impact on staff morale.

"We're looking for good ideas"

"If we work together we can make a difference"

"There may be some rewards and bonuses available"

"We'd like you all to get involved"

HOW TO...
PRESENT THE BUSINESS CASE FOR GOING GREEN

Explain to your staff that going green can bring real business benefits

↓

Describe the cost-effectiveness of short-term and mitigating measures, such as energy-saving

↓

Use case studies to highlight how other companies have benefited financially from making similar changes

↓

Discuss the long-term benefits of future-proofing – putting in place adaptation measures to the challenges your business is likely to face in the future

↓

Detail the PR benefits that going green will bring to your organization

Boosting morale

One of the most significant advantages of implementing a green business strategy, and one that is often cited by organizations that have already undergone the process, is that it can bring a noticeable improvement in the morale of your members of staff. We all want to feel as if we are "doing our bit" for the environment, and surveys have shown that employees working for businesses that are making serious efforts to minimize their environmental impact find their jobs more fulfilling as a consequence. In fact, the results are so striking that some organizations now regard going green as a talent attractor, because younger, more dynamic staff are likely to be drawn to firms that are more forward-thinking.

CASE STUDY

A productive move

When Genzyme Corporation was planning its new corporate headquarters in the US, it decided to make environmental sustainability a priority. The result was a 12-storey building that uses 42 per cent less energy and 34 per cent less water than comparable buildings. But, far more significantly, 58 per cent of the employees who work in the building report that they are more productive than they were in the previous headquarters. And – perhaps because the materials used in its construction were chosen on the basis that they emit fewer toxins – the amount of time lost through staff sickness in the building is five per cent lower than that of other Genzyme premises. Given that wages are a far larger percentage of a company's overall costs than energy, the financial benefits to the organization, as well as the advantages to employee morale, are clear.

Assessing yourself

The preliminary step to scrutinizing your business and the way in which it uses resources is to undergo a green audit. These thorough assessments will help you to define meaningful goals for your green strategy, and can be a very useful learning experience for your organization.

Taking a "green audit"

Green audits investigate your energy use, your water use, and your assets – they do the sums just like a financial assessment, but on an entirely new aspect of your business. Being audited is always an unnerving experience, but this is not like being audited by the tax office. You will not be penalized if shortcomings or failures are discovered. This is a positive audit, helping you to find ways to improve and streamline your operation. The detailed information you reap from such an audit will suggest new ways forward into the future, and will help you identify targets for improvement and set realistic goals to achieve.

Green auditing is a growing industry around the world. Some long-established consultancy firms are now retraining staff in this area, but there are also specialist green audit firms that focus only on sustainable issues. When choosing auditors to assess your business, make sure that the firm you hire has plenty of experience and a good track record.

CASE STUDY

Fans of energy saving
The Northern Irish organization Toughglass produces 4,000 square metres of glass a week and, after raw materials and wages, energy is its third-largest cost. Toughglass asked the UK government organization Carbon Trust (CT) to come in and assess its energy use. The CT's audit revealed that, as the glass was produced, the fans used to cool the glass as it came out of the furnaces could only operate at full capacity, and so the production process was using more energy than it needed to. The CT agreed to give Toughglass a loan in order to replace the old fans with newer models that have variable speed drives. This allowed much more control and brought the organization's costs down instantly, achieving an annual saving that covered the loan repayments more than threefold.

Choosing an audit

The focus of a green audit will vary depending on the type of business it is intended to assess. For heavy industries, for example, organizations may employ auditors to investigate energy use in their mines and plants and by their machinery, as well as the impacts of their transport systems, use of water, and systems for waste disposal. By contrast, for service-providing businesses such as insurance, tourism, and banking, the focus of a green audit is more likely to be on office-based energy use and waste, the working environment, and the impact of an organization's business activities on the environment. Consider taking expert advice to identify the areas of your operation that you would like your green audit to cover.

Once you have identified areas to focus on, there are various types of audit you can choose, including:
• **Energy audits** These help you reduce your CO_2 emissions by identifying the points at which your organization uses the most energy.
• **Waste audits** Pinpointing the sources of waste in your company will enable you to devise a waste reduction strategy.
• **Water audits** These identify areas in which you can reduce your water use.
• **Environmental systems audits** These help you construct an environmental management strategy by looking at the staff and management structures you already have in place.
• **Compliance audits** These ascertain whether all aspects of your business are fully compliant with regulatory requirements.

✓ CHECKLIST PREPARING FOR YOUR GREEN AUDIT

	YES	NO
• Have you fully explained the purpose of the audit to your staff?	☐	☐
• Have you asked staff to be completely honest when interviewed?	☐	☐
• Has a private room for the interviews been allocated?	☐	☐
• Have you let your staff know that the auditor's report will be widely available throughout the company? If there is any suspicion that you might be covering up the results, it will lead to a loss of morale.	☐	☐
• Are your staff confident that you will be addressing the problems that the audit uncovers?	☐	☐

Calculating your carbon footprint

*Carbon footprint
— the amount of
CO_2 emissions
produced annually
by an individual
or a company: their
"footprint" on the
atmosphere.

As climate change becomes a more serious threat, stakeholders and shareholders increasingly want to know that the organization they are investing in is taking steps to reduce its CO_2 emissions. The first step towards this is to undertake a special kind of audit that calculates the total emissions that a company is responsible for – its carbon footprint*. Like other types of audit, this information can be used to set targets for reducing emissions or even of going carbon neutral*.

*Carbon neutral —
reducing the net
amount of CO_2
emissions for
which a company
is responsible
to zero.

Accounting for emissions

There is still some dispute over the best way to measure a business's carbon footprint. The Greenhouse Gas Protocol provides an international standard for the emissions that should be included in your calculations. But it is up to the individual company and its auditor to select the systems by which those emissions are calculated, and the subtle differences between systems can lead to a variety of results.

A further difficulty lies in ensuring that emissions are counted only once. For example, auditors examining a car manufacturing company must decide who is responsible for the emissions produced by the disposal of the car. Is it the manufacturer, the consumer, or the waste disposal company? European manufacturers bear legal responsibility for the disposal of their goods, but does this extend to the carbon emissions? There are, as yet, no simple answers to these questions: carbon footprints are an inexact science, currently being refined through practice.

Footprinting products

It is becoming increasingly popular to apply the concept of carbon footprinting to individual products. Putting a carbon footprint label on your goods is a useful way of demonstrating your commitment to reducing your emissions. The Canadian firm Carbon Counted and the UK Carbon Trust have led the way with carbon footprint labelling, and it is now mandatory for some goods under European law. The giant US retail chain Wal-Mart has teamed up with the Carbon Disclosure Project to measure the footprints of seven different product categories – beer, DVDs, toothpaste, soap, milk, vacuum cleaners, and carbonated drinks – not so that it could label them, but so that it could look at ways of reducing their footprints.

A parallel practice is Life-cycle Analysis (LCA). Carbon footprinting only measures the emissions to the point of sale: LCA looks at the emissions produced either by extracting or manufacturing the product's raw materials, as well as emissions from transportation, packaging, manufacture, storage, the product's use, and its disposal.

IN FOCUS... CONSUMER FOOTPRINTS

The majority of the carbon footprint of a product arises during its use by the person who has purchased it – the consumer. The retail environment offers real possibilities for influencing consumer behaviour and so taking steps towards reducing this footprint. Opening discussions with your customers to encourage them to change the way they use your product can work well. For example, for a firm that sells fabric detergent, encouraging customers to reduce the temperature of their washes is a really effective way of reducing the overall carbon footprint of the product.

Reducing your energy use

Reducing the amount of energy used is central to any business's green strategy. Anyone who has walked through a city at night and seen the office blocks sparkling throughout the small hours knows that organizations can have a very wasteful attitude to energy. This not only adds to our impact on the environment, but also to our bills.

TIP

CHECK YOUR NIGHT USAGE

Take a meter reading at the end of the day, and then again the following morning before work begins. The difference is energy wasted while no-one is working.

Saving energy in your office

You can start saving energy in the office even before the auditors arrive. Take a walk around your office space looking for places in which you are wasting energy, or opportunities for changing equipment or practices to make energy savings. Repeat these "energy inspections" regularly to monitor progress, and to spot new energy-saving possibilities. Remember that small actions can achieve a great deal. Reducing your energy bill may be as simple as setting the heating thermostat a little lower in winter, or cutting back on use of air-conditioning in summer.

✔ CHECKLIST ASSESSING THE ENERGY EFFICIENCY OF YOUR OFFICE

	YES	NO
• Are our computer systems, photocopiers, faxes, and telephones the most energy-efficient models available?	☐	☐
• Are all energy-efficiency modes of office equipment enabled?	☐	☐
• Does anyone have responsibility for ensuring that lights and equipment are switched off at the end of the day?	☐	☐
• Do we use energy-efficient light bulbs?	☐	☐
• Is the building well insulated?	☐	☐
• Are the boilers modern and efficient?	☐	☐
• Is the heating timer set to switch off overnight?	☐	☐
• Does our external lighting switch on only as the sun sets?	☐	☐

Monitoring your IT system

It is estimated that the IT industry is responsible for two per cent of global CO_2 emissions, so any energy review should start with your computer systems. Attaching mini-meters to different parts of your systems in order to identify the most power-hungry items can often result in significant energy savings. And if you are considering installing a new system, look at those produced by organizations that are working to improve the efficiency of their models and undertaking research to find ways of reducing their server energy consumption.

TIP

USE MOTIVATIONAL METHODS

Use incentives and competitions to make saving energy fun – this can be good for staff morale and will help you achieve energy savings more quickly.

Buying green energy

Consider using a green energy supplier. There are many options now available, including energy companies that provide energy solely from renewable sources, and others that use traditional methods, such as coal-fired plants, but make a commitment to invest in building new renewable sources. Most of the large power companies now offer a green tariff of some kind – at a slightly higher cost than the standard tariff. The energy that is supplied to you will not come directly from renewable sources, but the company offsets the amount of energy that you use against energy that they have obtained from renewable sources. Be careful to check the details, as some tariffs may not be as green as they first appear.

Monitoring energy use in industry

TIP

MAKE SOMEONE RESPONSIBLE

Who looks after the energy bills at your plant? Giving the task of reducing energy usage to someone who is at the plant itself often makes savings quicker and easier to achieve than if it is managed off-site at a head office.

Nearly 20 per cent of all global greenhouse gases are produced by industrial energy use. Industries such as the chemical industry, the cement industry, and the petroleum-refinery industry are particularly carbon-heavy. Energy savings made by reduction, replacement, and innovation are vital to cut this sizeable carbon footprint. In Europe, several industry sectors are already obligated to take part in the European Union Greenhouse Gas Emissions Trading Scheme, which sets limits on the CO_2 emissions an organization can be responsible for. In the US, some organizations are joining voluntary schemes for carbon reporting, such as the Chicago Climate Exchange.

Large industrial businesses often need specialist help when attempting to reduce the amount of energy they use. Some governments provide advice services that will take businesses through a thorough assessment process and offer suggestions as to how savings can be made. These bodies can be particularly useful because they often have access to grant money to fund energy-saving changes. However, if your government does not offer a suitable service, there are plenty of private companies with expertise in this area.

IN FOCUS... ENERGY FOR SHOPPING

Retail space is more energy-intensive than either offices or factories. A study carried out in 2007 estimated that retailers, on average, use 460 kilowatt hours (kWh) annually per square metre, considerably more than that used by factories (292kWh) and commercial offices (252kWh). Special solutions are needed to reduce the excessive retail use of energy. One large supermarket chain estimates that most of the energy used by its stores is for refrigeration and is investigating alternatives. Open-door policies – in which shops leave their doors open at all times – can be a source of waste, and so some retailers, such as the international fast-food chain McDonald's, have a policy of keeping their doors closed.

Saving energy

Are there any changes you could make to reduce the amount of energy your plant uses?

- **Improve your housekeeping** Is your machinery kept in the best and most efficient condition? Is maintenance carried out regularly? Mending leaks in compressed air and refrigeration systems will lead to energy savings. Keeping filters clean will improve their operation.

- **Replace old machinery** Are there newer models that would be more efficient? Would the savings offset the cost of replacement?

- **Use equipment less** Is machinery used where non-mechanical solutions would be less energy-intensive and more effective?

- **Conserve heat** Could heat generated by your machinery be captured and used for other purposes, such as heating water?

- **Limit unnecessary operation** Are machines running during breaks, or when they are not needed?

- **Turn down your heating** Are heating controls on machinery set higher than they need to be?

- **Check your meter** How efficient is your energy metering? Modern meters can reveal detailed information about energy use and help you identify ways to make reductions.

- **Replace your boiler** Could you upgrade your boiler system to one that is more energy-efficient?

Minimizing waste

The case for reducing the amount of waste your organization produces on a day-to-day basis is compelling. It is clear for any business that high wastage means high costs. So finding ways to reduce the waste you produce is just good, simple business sense.

Streamlining your approach

*Extended Producer Responsibility — *you make it, you clear it up: the producer bears responsibility for the disposal of the goods it sells.*

Waste is often a forgotten cost: the price of over-ordering materials or discarding them because of poor design or workmanship is just absorbed into the price. Take a rigorous approach to your waste: include it as a factor in your costs right from the beginning and look for ways to reduce it. This doesn't stop at the point of sale of your product: voluntary Extended Producer Responsibility* commitments mean that firms are increasingly looking into consumer use of their products and how they are disposed of.

To minimize your waste, adopt three principles: reduce, reuse, and recycle. Before you discard anything, think: did we need to use it in the first place? Is there any way that we can reuse it? If not, how can we best recycle it?

CASE STUDY

McDonald's Sweden

In the 1990s, the Managing Director of McDonald's Sweden became concerned about the environmental impact of the company. He decided to radically rethink the way that the organization operated, and put in place a painstaking analysis and reform strategy. The first change made was to source meat, milk, and vegetables from organic suppliers. The company also reduced its distribution distances, introduced environmentally friendly packaging, and began running its headquarters and many of its stores on renewable energy. Most drastic of all of the reforms, however, was a waste sorting and recycling campaign, which has seen a 97 per cent reduction in the amount of waste produced: the average Swedish McDonald's store now sends one bag of unsorted waste a month to landfill.

Making reductions

Cutting your waste starts with reduction, which simply means either not using something, or using less of it. It is easier than it seems, but the idea needs to be factored in from the beginning of any process, and continually referred back to throughout.

In construction, for example, costs can often be reduced if the points at which waste will occur are identified early on, and solutions found. This could include making less complicated designs using the same materials throughout as far as possible, for example, rather than different materials for every part of the building. It could mean a design using resources already in place, such as stocks of timber or stone already held by the construction company. Procurement is an important area in which waste can be reduced: inaccurate estimates can lead to materials being over-ordered, and then not used and discarded. Product packaging can also lead to unnecessary waste material: are there ways in which you can cut down on the amount of packaging needed to protect and display your products?

TIP

COUNT THE TOTAL COST

Remember to calculate the true cost of your waste: include the cost of removal, the original cost of the materials, and the cost of the manpower needed to get rid of it.

Reduce

Two ways in which firms are reducing their waste, and their bills: a fabric detergent manufacturer began selling its fabric detergent in a more concentrated form, in smaller bottles. It saves on the waste generated, raw materials used, and the amount of fuel needed to transport the product. A company that refines magnesite ore into magnesium oxide found that it was losing raw material at a magnetic filter stage. It changed the magnet in the filter and reduced both its waste and its raw material needs.

IN FOCUS...
ZERO WASTE

Increasingly, companies are announcing targets of zero waste: using the three basic principles of reduction, reuse, and recycling to shrink the amount of waste they send to landfill to zero. Several major organizations, including Wal-Mart, General Motors, and Toyota, for example, have announced zero waste targets in the future for all or part of their operations. These programmes will require complete rethinks of the entire businesses and, in some areas, serious innovation, but if they are successful, they will significantly reduce their impact on the environment.

Reusing materials

It is surprising how often a perfectly useful object is discarded without a moment's thought, when it could be useful for another purpose in exactly the same form. A classic example can be seen in the construction industry: building firms traditionally tear down houses, dispose of the materials, and then buy in a new load of bricks, tiles, and fixtures and fittings to go in their place.

Take a careful look at what your organization throws away every day: if you can find creative ways of reusing materials that would otherwise be discarded, you will not only save on the cost of buying new materials, but also on the cost of removing the old materials and any landfill charges.

Reuse

Two ways in which firms are reusing waste, and saving money:
• A firm that manufactures kitchen cabinets was producing a large quantity of timber waste that wasn't suitable for reuse. It installed a wood-burning boiler and began to use its waste wood in it, reducing its heating bills.
• An international fast food company turns the fat used to fry chips into biodiesel, which it uses to power its vehicles. The company not only saves on fuel bills, but also reduces the costs of disposing of its food waste.

Encouraging recycling

You can always find someone who will argue that recycling is more wasteful than just binning a product. "What about the energy used up in collecting it?", they say. "What if it all gets taken across the globe?" In fact, a number of scientific studies have shown that recycling leads to considerable savings in energy and resources: the energy saved by recycling one glass bottle instead of throwing it away, for example, will power a computer for 20 minutes.

Offices are a significant source of unnecessary waste: millions of tonnes of discarded paper that could be recycled are sent from offices to landfill every year. Retailers that persuade their customers to recycle, and that recycle themselves, are also contributing to a significant reduction in waste.

The market for recycled materials is growing rapidly – the use of recycled materials for aggregate in the construction industry, for example, is becoming more and more widespread.

Meanwhile, regulations are starting to come into play that give producers responsibility for what happens to their goods at the end of their working life. In the electronic goods sector, Xerox have led the way in finding creative solutions to recycling old products. The company encourages its customers to return old products, and is committed to reusing components from this old machinery in new products – a process known as "remanufacturing".

Recycle

Two innovative ways in which firms are recycling their waste:
• A large construction project, building two carriageways as part of an airport complex, used locally sourced crushed glass and recycled local aggregate, cutting the cost of transporting aggregate from further afield.
• A chain of lighting retailers asked its customers to bring back used light bulbs to be recycled. This encouraged customers back into the shop, increasing the chance they would buy replacement light bulbs there too.

Tackling transport

Transport as a whole is responsible for a large proportion of global CO_2 emissions, and so needs to be a key part of your green strategy. Consider ways to reduce the amount of business travel you do, or come up with transport alternatives that will reduce your carbon footprint.

Understanding the problem

Our increasingly global businesses often have a very high mileage, from the delivery of raw materials and products to daily commuter journeys and overseas business trips. Road freight, for example, accounts for nearly 10 per cent of CO_2 emissions in some developed countries. Commuter miles are increasing, and in some countries most workers commute by car and travel alone. In others, car use is still unusual but growing rapidly. Air travel is a particular problem. As plane fares drop and journey times shorten, so air passenger numbers have increased year on year. Aeroplanes pump out more CO_2 per passenger than most other forms of travel, and other gases emitted by aircraft high into the atmosphere also contribute to global warming, potentially doubling each aircraft's contribution to climate change.

train*
116kg

small car*
124kg

coach*
172kg

Choosing solutions

Fortunately, businesses are starting to come up with innovative ways to reduce the impact of their travel needs. Examples include:
• **Using rail transport** Although the routes available are less flexible than transport by road, rail has far lower energy costs. It can also often be faster and allow greater quantities of goods to be transported.
• **Transporting goods by water** In countries in which there is already a network of canals and rivers, using water transport can considerably cut energy costs and alleviate road congestion. However, it is less flexible and often slower than road transport.
• **Re-routing** Using high-tech navigational programmes and intelligent fuel monitoring, as well as redesigning routes and haulier systems to maximize efficiency, involves some initial cost, but can generate significant fuel savings.

• **Reducing commuter miles** Lift-share schemes can be set up to enable staff that get to work by car to make arrangements to travel together. Some organizations encourage staff to leave their cars at home by subsidizing train and bus passes, or installing secure bike sheds and shower facilities.
• **Minimizing air travel** Frequent flyers can plan creatively, to use the train where possible, and to combine meetings or stay longer so that they reduce the number of flights they need to take. Some firms remove the need for overseas travel entirely by holding meetings via video-conferencing, which allows audio and video communication across the internet between two or more locations.
• **Using partnerships** A voluntary US transport partnership scheme compels firms that sign up to it to work towards reducing emissions and report on their results, in return for being able to display its logo.

large car*

248kg

plane*

306kg

*Amount of CO_2 produced by two people travelling a distance of 600 miles

Monitoring your supply chain

A green audit will look at your own organization and how you can save energy or reduce waste, but it usually will not take into account the practices of your suppliers. Check your supply chain – sometimes the highest savings can be made in the most unexpected places.

Assessing your suppliers

Sustainability should permeate every aspect of your business, beginning with the products and services that you choose. Talk to your suppliers about their company policies: do they have a green strategy for their business? Are they working to reduce their CO_2 emissions and the amount of waste they produce? Find out whether they get their raw materials from sustainable sources, and whether they have looked into the environmental practices of their own suppliers. If you are not fully satisfied with their answers, discuss working with them to improve their practices, or seek out a new supplier.

✔ CHECKLIST **CHOOSING MATERIALS**

	YES	NO
• Does your organization really need the materials?	☐	☐
• How often are they used – could they be borrowed or rented?	☐	☐
• Do they use the minimum amount of packaging necessary?	☐	☐
• Are the CO_2 emissions and waste produced during their manufacture as low as possible?	☐	☐
• Are the materials the most energy-efficient option available?	☐	☐
• Are they made locally? (Not having to be transported over long distances means lower CO_2 emissions and less pollution.)	☐	☐
• How will they be disposed of – can they be recycled?	☐	☐
• Do they contain the maximum recycled or reused content possible?	☐	☐
• Are they a naturally occurring, renewable, and sustainable resource?	☐	☐

Using green logos and labels

If you are looking for a new supplier or new premises, you will want to be sure that they have the right green credentials. There are a large number of logos and labels used by firms to demonstrate their greenness. These fall, very simply, into two types: those that indicate a certified, independently audited standard, and those that do not. Certified labels are usually either produced by governments or charities: participation is almost always voluntary, although this may change as environmental requirements increase. Examples include the Forestry Stewardship Council logo, which is used to certify timber that has been grown and harvested sustainably, and the BRE Environmental Assessment Method (BREEAM) and Leadership in Energy and Environmental Design (LEED) certification schemes, which give clear information about the environmental friendliness of a building. By contrast, labels that are set up voluntarily by groups of businesses and that are not independently audited and certified may sometimes simply be examples of greenwash*.

*Greenwash — *unsubstantiated claims that are intended to make a company look greener than it really is.*

CASE STUDY

Crisping up

When potato crisp company Walkers Crisps was assessed by the Carbon Trust to look for possible savings in its carbon emissions, the Trust spotted an opportunity to make what it called a market correction. Walkers purchase large quantities of potatoes, and pay the farmers for them by weight. Farmers store their potatoes in artificially humidified sheds, which adds to the water content of the potatoes and makes them heavier: however the extra water content increases the amount of time that Walkers then has to fry them. The Carbon Trust suggested that Walkers should make arrangements with farmers to pay more for potatoes with lower water content, rather than by weight. This simple change saves emissions from both the farms and from Walkers' fryers.

Choosing sustainable finance

Finance is central to any business, and can also be an important part of your green strategy. Check out the green credentials of your financial providers. Could you switch to companies that employ ethical investment strategies for your pension plans and savings schemes?

TIP

THINK ABOUT THE WIDER BENEFITS

Switching to an ethical pension or investment policy can be good PR and useful for your image: employees and NGOs like to know where an organization's money is going.

Understanding ethical options

In response to an increasing demand for investment options that are not only financially successful, but also socially and environmentally responsible, the worldwide ethical finance market has seen extraordinary growth. There is now a wide range of investment products available that limit investment to organizations that fit a chosen set of ethical and environmental criteria. These include green issues, such as energy reduction targets; governance issues, such as corporate social policy; and social issues – whether a company is involved in arms or gambling, for example.

ASSESSING ETHICAL INVESTMENTS

STRATEGY	HOW IT WORKS	PROS	CONS
Positive screening	Firms are chosen for investment on the basis that their products and services are ethically "positive" – for example, that they generate renewable energy or manufacture vaccines.	Only those companies that meet positive criteria are selected.	Choice for investment is limited.
Preference	A list of guidelines is drawn up, relating to work practices or environmental record, for example. Firms chosen for investment must be the closest fit to those criteria.	This gives a broad spectrum of firms, but is not as inclusive as the "engagement" approach.	Firms that don't fully meet an investor's personal criteria may still be included.
Engagement	Rather than just excluding any firm on the grounds of its activities, fund managers actively try to engage with that firm to see if they can extract promises of improvement.	This encourages firms to improve their environmental record.	Funds may be invested with companies that don't fit the criteria of the investor.
Negative screening	Firms are blacklisted if they operate in specified industries, such as gambling or tobacco.	Specific "undesirable" industries will be excluded.	May exclude some profitable sectors; does not actively encourage improvement.

Exploring green banking options

Some banks are more environmentally friendly or socially responsible than others, so it is worth taking time to investigate a financial provider's green credentials before you make the decision to give them your business. The international bank HSBC, for example, is committed to reducing its impact on the environment, and became carbon neutral in 2005. European bank Triodos is probably the greenest of all: it will lend money only to people and projects that directly benefit the environment.

Chapter 3

Communicating the message

How should you let people know about your greening plans? Some businesses have not publicized them, while others have blazoned their initiatives to the world. Use imagination and sensitivity to choose the path that is best for your organization.

Capturing green consumers

Consumer demand is the one crucial factor that will persuade businesses that they have to become more green. Customers are increasingly seeking out firms that are greener and products that are more ethically produced, and businesses that pay attention to this will profit.

Meeting demand

Some businesses remain unconvinced of the need to be greener. They draw attention to surveys that show that although customers may tell focus groups they want greener products, their actions when shopping do not necessarily match their words.

But the fact is that consumer concern about the environmental impacts of the products and services they buy is growing. Surveys show a rapid growth in awareness of greener products, and demand is increasing. Businesses that do not respond may be left behind by more forward-thinking competitors.

Spreading the word

More and more companies are making the transition to a green way of working. But how do you let your clients and customers know you have taken these steps? For a long time, many of the world's greenest organizations chose not to advertise their green credentials, fearing that they would open themselves up to criticism in other areas, or that it would win them little market advantage.

IKEA, for example, spent 12 years implementing a green business strategy, but decided in 2002 that it would not use this for advertising purposes. The company did, however, make its records available to anyone who wanted to know – from NGOs to members of the public. In 2007, IKEA was placed seventh in a major US ranking of the greenest companies, beating many organizations that had spent a great deal on advertising their greenness.

However, the situation is changing. As awareness of environmental impacts continues to be absorbed into the mainstream, it will become more important for firms to be able to demonstrate that they have the proper credentials as standard. Advertising your carbon and waste reductions may not lead to a direct increase in the sales of your goods or services, but it will certainly augment the reputation of your organization, and in the current climate, this might just give you an edge on the competition.

CASE STUDY

Doing the right thing

In the early 2000s, shoe company Timberland made a radical decision to measure its environmental and ethical impacts and present the results to the public with a "Green Index" – a rating that graded its products based on their carbon footprints. But it was not doing this in response to demands from focus groups or surveys, or because the company thought it would sell more shoes. It was doing it because, as the European Director Anabel Drese put it, "it was right".

Avoiding greenwash

Today's consumer is extremely well educated in the various marketing techniques used to sell brands, and can be suspicious and cynical of green claims. As a result, even the most honest campaign can fall prey to cries of "greenwash" – the suggestion that the claims being made are exaggerated, misleading, or simply not true.

Getting the message across

If you do decide that you want to advertise your green policies, how can you minimize the risk of your claims being labelled as greenwash? Firstly, and most importantly, you need to make sure that every claim you make is true. Before planning a campaign, make sure you are familiar with all aspects of the product or service, and with any environmental arguments or controversies that could be relevant to your claims. Ask yourself whether it is a product or service that really deserves to be marketed as green: is it representative of ongoing environmental development in your organization? Or might consumers perceive it as a token gesture? Consider working in partnership with an NGO or charity – this can be a very useful way of getting independent endorsement for your campaign.

SIN OF FIBBING
Making an environmental claim that is verifiably untrue: claiming to be organic, for example, when the company is not certified.

CASE STUDY

A successful partnership

When the European rail company Eurostar sent out press releases about the fact that it had gone carbon neutral, it included a quote from Tony Juniper, the head of environmental charity Friends of the Earth (FoE), indicating his approval of the actions. Eurostar had taken an extremely thorough approach to going green, and had reduced its energy use significantly before resorting to buying carbon offsets; this meant that FoE were happy to endorse its work.

The six sins of greenwashing

The most typical greenwashing mistakes have been defined by US environmental marketing organization TerraChoice:

SIN OF LESSER OF TWO EVILS
Making an environmental claim that may be true but is not much use in the context: for example, marketing a motor vehicle with extremely high fuel consumption as having energy-efficient air-conditioning.

SIN OF IRRELEVANCE
Making an environmental claim that is no longer relevant: for example, chlorofluorocarbons (CFCs) have been banned since the late 1980s, but products such as shaving gels are still occasionally marketed as being "CFC-free".

SIN OF NO PROOF
Making an environmental claim without providing any certification or proof to back that claim up: for example, claiming that a shampoo has not been tested on animals but offering no independent verification.

SIN OF VAGUENESS
Making an environmental claim that has no specific meaning: for example, promoting a food item as "natural", or "wholesome".

SIN OF THE HIDDEN TRADE-OFF
Suggesting that a product is green based on a single environmental attribute: advertising that an office printer is energy efficient, for example, without mentioning that it is incompatible with recycled toner cartridges.

Reporting and marketing

The business world is increasingly finding that consumers want transparency from the organizations they deal with. They feel – with some justification – that because they provide an organization's profit they also have the right to know how that profit is generated.

Taking responsibility

The first step towards a transparent approach to business is to examine how you communicate your aims and report on your progress. In the past 15 years, there has been a huge increase in the visibility of Corporate Social Responsibility (CSR) policies. Organizations publically state a set of green and ethical CSR commitments, displaying them prominently on their websites and in public documents. Progress towards achieving these goals is published periodically in CSR reports that are made widely available. This can be a very effective way of letting customers and investors know about your green progress, but it must reflect a genuine desire within your organization to improve or you could open yourself up to criticism. The global oil firm Shell, for example, has made much of its CSR policy, but some NGOs and consumers believe that this is incompatible with its continuing legal action against the court order to cease flaring – burning off the natural gas that is produced during oil refining – in Nigeria.

IN FOCUS...

DEALING WITH CAMPAIGNS

Even businesses with the clearest reporting systems can sometimes find themselves the focus of a green campaign. Handled correctly, however, this can be turned into a positive and useful experience. Rather than trying to ignore the demands of the campaigners, talk to them. Invite them in to look around your operation and listen to what they say. Can you accommodate their demands? Consider whether the impact of any negative publicity associated with their campaign would outweigh the financial costs of making some or all of the changes they are calling for.

Gaining certification

Having your CSR or progress report audited by an international organisation in order to be certified gives your work credibility. The gold standard of environmental certification is ISO14001, produced by the International Organization for Standardization (ISO). This specifies a framework for environmental management systems against which an organization is certified, and is recognized internationally. While international take-up of ISO14001 is increasing globally, it is showing most growth in Asia, where businesses producing goods for Western markets are obtaining certification in order to meet pre-set standards for the firms they are supplying. ISO also produces standards for other areas, including sustainability, environmental labelling and auditing, and greenhouse gas management.

PREPARE FOR CERTIFICATION

When applying for ISO certification, first ensure you read and understand the standard; gain commitment and backing of senior managers; and attend training courses designed to help you implement and assess your environmental management system.

HOW TO...
AVOID PROBLEMS WITH CSR REPORTS

Don't cherry pick – choosing only the successes you want to highlight and ignoring less attractive results	Set out the area you are going to cover early on and then stick to that structure; use independent auditors to verify results
Be completely honest – don't bury bad news, such as failure to hit a carbon- or waste-reduction target	If you are genuinely trying to reach your targets, people will understand that sometimes you will encounter setbacks
Give the right impression – don't fall prey to the accusation that you are "sugar coating" a purely profit-making motive	Tell it straight: state the business reasons for going green as clearly as you do the environmental benefits
Be persuasive – address those who argue that it is not the job of organizations to take on environmental and social responsibilities	Make the case that businesses must play their part, as the financial cost of not acting will be much greater

TIP

STAY ON THE RIGHT TRACK
Remember that your main aim is to reduce your environmental impact. Don't let marketing take precedence over genuine action.

Marketing yourself

CSR commitments and reports will reach those customers interested enough in your business to visit your website or investigate your literature, but there are many ways to let the wider public know about the changes you have been making to your organization. Green marketing guru John Grant has divided the various actions you can choose to get your green message across into three main categories:

• **Setting new standards** Fixing a higher bar for your own behaviour, such as promising that in future all raw materials will be sustainably sourced.

• **Sharing responsibility** Asking consumers to play their own part – encouraging recycling of your product's packaging, for example.

• **Supporting innovation** Exploring and promoting technological advances that reduce the impact of your business on the environment.

Within these categories, marketing actions can range from pledges and events to campaigns and green partnerships. The approaches that are right for your business will depend largely on the message you are aiming to get across. However you choose to market your green message, bear in mind that if you are challenging yourself and your organization to truly shift to a more progressive agenda, then you will be making the kinds of decisions that the public respect.

IN FOCUS... CHECK YOUR DETAILS

When you market yourself as green, you make yourself a potential hostage: if there is a single detail of your marketing strategy that is not consistent with your central message, you risk the campaign backfiring, and your organization looking either hypocritical or stupid. So if you are organizing a green event and handing out gift bags, for example, put the gifts in a cotton bag, not a plastic one, and don't give away something made from plastic and imported from the other side of the world.

GREEN MARKETING OPTIONS

ACTION	EXAMPLE	PROS AND CONS
Cause-related marketing Ally yourself to a good cause. Sponsor a charity event or give money to a good cause for a specific product sold.	In 2006, UK cosmetics firm Lush launched its Charity Pot Handcream. It donated all proceeds (except the VAT) to environmental campaign groups.	**Pros** Makes customers feel involved and good about themselves. **Cons** Some purchase-triggered donations don't result in a large amount going to the charity, so your campaign could be labelled as greenwash.
Green partnerships Secure the endorsement of one of the larger NGOs or charities, for either a product or a programme.	Malaysian palm oil producer Sime Darby is working with the World Wildlife Fund and the Roundtable on Sustainable Palm Oil to increase the sustainability of its business.	**Pros** The public trust these organizations, so will be more likely to believe your claims. **Cons** The NGO or charity will want to be fully satisfied with your green strategy, so you may need to give them more access to your business than you find comfortable.
Advertising campaigns Use print, television, radio, or web advertisements to market yourself as green.	The car manufacturer Honda uses advertising to market itself very heavily as a green pioneer.	**Pros** Directly lets your customers know what you are doing. **Cons** If your green credentials are not completely watertight, running an advertising campaign could backfire and attract negative publicity.
Make green second tier Employ an advertising strategy that markets a green product, but concentrates on other desirable attributes of it, such as its quality or durability.	US outdoor clothing firm Patagonia has radical environmental policies, but markets its products on the durability and technical advantages of its gear.	**Pros** Markets your goods on a less-difficult selling point, while still getting the information about your environmental work to the public. **Cons** The product needs to function well on two fronts.
Green innovation Develop an innovative green product to show that you are a pioneer in your field.	The satellite television company British Sky Broadcasting has developed set-top decoder boxes that automatically switch to standby if left on.	**Pros** Shows that you are innovative, responsible, and serious about the issues. **Cons** This is an expensive option that could backfire if the innovation is deemed to be a superficial solution, rather than a serious attempt to deal with a problem.

Engaging consumers

Consumers have their own set of environmental responsibilities, and as a business, you should engage with your customers about the ways in which they can affect change too. If you handle this sensitively, this course of action can be the most effective of all.

TIP

PUSH THE BOUNDARIES

Don't be afraid of making radical decisions on behalf of your customers. If the decision you have made is right, they will come along with you.

Taking a lead

For most products – from cars and computers to washing-up liquid – it is during use by consumers that the majority of their environmental impact occurs. So although it is vital that your firm makes every effort to reduce the environmental impact of its own activities, it is also crucial to open up lines of communication with consumers about the way they are using your products. Choose your tone carefully, however, as no-one likes to be told what they should and should not do.

Getting labelling right

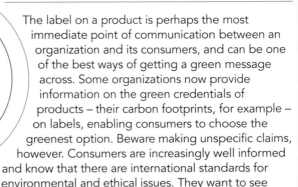

The label on a product is perhaps the most immediate point of communication between an organization and its consumers, and can be one of the best ways of getting a green message across. Some organizations now provide information on the green credentials of products – their carbon footprints, for example – on labels, enabling consumers to choose the greenest option. Beware making unspecific claims, however. Consumers are increasingly well informed and know that there are international standards for environmental and ethical issues. They want to see you meet those standards, not just invent your own.

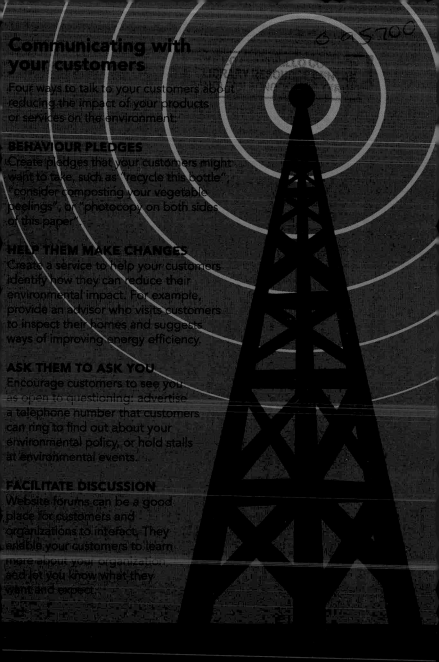

Communicating with your customers

Four ways to talk to your customers about reducing the impact of your products or services on the environment.

BEHAVIOUR PLEDGES
Create pledges that your customers might want to take, such as "recycle this bottle", "consider composting your vegetable peelings", or "photocopy on both sides of this paper".

HELP THEM MAKE CHANGES
Create a service to help your customers identify how they can reduce their environmental impact. For example, provide an advisor who visits customers to inspect their homes and suggests ways of improving energy efficiency.

ASK THEM TO ASK YOU
Encourage customers to see you as open to questioning: advertise a telephone number that customers can ring to find out about your environmental policy, or hold stalls at environmental events.

FACILITATE DISCUSSION
Website forums can be a good place for customers and organizations to interact. They enable your customers to learn more about your organization, and let you know what they want and expect.

Chapter 4

Preparing for the future

In the next few decades, the business environment is going to change. Technology is developing fast, legislation and reporting duties are increasing, and there is a growing range of opportunities opening up for forward-thinking businesses.

Adapting to change

If you are not thinking about the impact that environmental change may have on your business, you are not planning properly for the future. As the climate of the earth changes, adapting to a new physical environment will be one of the major challenges an organization has to face.

Anticipating wild weather

Over the last decade, evidence has grown that the warming of the climate will lead to an increase in unpredictable and extreme weather. We are already seeing an increase in freak weather events. Europe experienced a severe heat wave in 2003, in which over 30,000 people died; in the US in 2005, Hurricane Katrina devastated the city of New Orleans in Louisiana; and Australia suffered a serious drought during the 2006–2007 summer. Scientists predict that violent fluctuations in the weather such as these will become regular events as the climate changes.

Facing challenges

The insurance industry was amongst the first to realise the risk the changing climate poses to its business and has long been calling for mitigative and adaptive action on the part of governments. Its calls are now backed by many large businesses, and in some countries government agencies are beginning to offer advice on the difficulties that climate change may present. In the UK, for example, the UK Climate Impact Programme (UKCIP) offers organizations assessment tools to help plan for the impacts of climate change on business. In China, the Ministry for Science and Technology is carrying out an investigation into the impacts of climate change in rural China, which will eventually result in an adaptation framework.

ADAPTATION MEASURES – PREPARING FOR CLIMATE CHANGE

CHALLENGE	AREAS TO CONSIDER	POSSIBLE TACTICS
Extreme heat	Does your organization have mechanisms to deal with a heat wave? How would staff cope? Would your production be affected?	Install natural ventilation systems, indoor water features, or architectural cooling features.
Drought	Is your business water dependent? Can you call on reserves in times of shortage?	Construct a small reservoir; back up with stock that is less water-dependent.
Floods and storms	Is your business vulnerable to flooding or storm damage? Do you have evacuation plans and alternative storage facilities? In extreme flood scenarios the sewerage systems in some cities may fail – would this place your business at further risk?	Flood-proof your buildings; look for storage facilities on high ground; ensure that you have an efficient back-up system for electronic data.
Power cuts	Extreme weather events may lead to power cuts. Do you have a secondary supply? Would goods be affected if there was a prolonged outage?	Make sure you have back-up power supplies on hand; drill staff in what to do if the power cuts out.
Fuel shortages	How would shortages of fuel affect your business? Would it prevent staff from coming in? Would it affect your distribution networks?	Investigate ways to cut down on fuel use; consider storing back-up supplies for emergency use.

Keeping up with technology

Keep your eyes open for new ideas to save and create energy and lower emissions of greenhouse gases. Technological advances are offering new opportunities for astute businesses to make savings, be it using wind-powered freight ships or air-powered motorbikes.

Being ready for the future

The long-term success of the human race has been built on being able to adapt to the ever-changing circumstances it finds itself in. In the next 20 years, as the climate changes and resources start to become less plentiful, those adaptive skills are going to be called on time and time again. Businesses will need to start looking forward and grasping the future. Those that can afford to spend large amounts of money on research and development and lead in the development of green technologies will reap the rewards. But for all businesses, remaining aware of the latest developments and embracing the use of new technologies will ensure that they are best equipped to succeed. Those that fail to adapt and lag behind the field are likely to lose out.

 IN FOCUS... CUT AND SWITCH

Businesses that are seeking to reduce their environmental impact have, in most cases, a choice of two paths they can take. Firstly, they can make changes that reduce the impact of their current activities, such as turning lights off when they are not in use. This approach leads to a reduction in the amount of energy that the business uses. Alternatively, they can switch technologies, such as powering their lights by solar power instead of mains electricity. These approaches are not mutually exclusive, and it is likely to be a combination of both that will lead to the quickest reduction in the amount of energy used.

Finding solutions

Keeping up with the latest advances in green technology isn't easy – this is a rapidly growing field and major developments are reported daily. Keep an open mind and think creatively – the opportunities available to your business may not be immediately obvious and straightforward. A good example of this type of innovative thinking can be seen in Sweden. A system is being built in Stockholm railway station that captures the body heat produced by the passengers and uses it to heat a neighbouring office system. The office's heating bills will be reduced by 15 per cent.

Thinking ahead

Innovations such as this call for a long-term, cyclical approach to business, as they require a fairly large upfront cost. It may take many years of reduced heating bills to compensate for the investment required for the installation of solar panels, for example. For this reason, larger organizations find it easier to decide to invest in new technology than smaller businesses with less leeway in their financial plans. But when deciding whether to invest, think carefully about the long-term implications of being left behind.

HOW TO...
KEEP UP WITH THE LATEST DEVELOPMENTS

Sign up to a green business newsletter, such as the E-newsletter on www.climatebiz.com, that reports on the latest green business innovations.

↓

Attend green business conferences: they are invaluable places for getting up-to-date information, and meeting and speaking to people face-to-face.

↓

Subscribe to general scientific and business magazines that report on environmental issues.

↓

Some of the independent environmental websites, such as www.treehugger.com, include updates on inventions and pilots that may be of use.

↓

Investigate whether your government has a department that supports green innovation, and ask them to add you to their mailing list.

↓

Finally, keep your eyes open: you can never predict where you'll find inspiration. It could be in a women's glossy magazine, or simply while you're walking down the street.

Using renewable energy

Although the idea of renewable energy has been floating around for centuries, big business has only just woken up to the possibilities, and money is starting to pour into the sector. As the technology advances, there will be more and more options for using sustainable energy sources to power businesses, so keep your eyes open for the latest developments.

Knowing your options

*Fossil fuels —
non-renewable
resources, including
coal, oil, and gas,
made over millions
of years from the
organic remains of
prehistoric plants
and animals, which,
when burnt,
release energy.*

The generation of electricity from fossil fuels* is one of the major sources of CO_2 emissions. It is also unsustainable: fossil fuels are a finite resource, and long before they run out, they will become uneconomic to extract. By contrast, renewable energy – energy derived ultimately from the power of the sun, for example, or from the heat trapped beneath the earth's crust – is effectively limitless, though unlike fossil fuels, it is very diffuse and hard to gather and concentrate. Our energy future is likely to include a mixture of renewable sources, though it is not yet clear which technologies will prevail.

TIDES
Turbines are installed in areas with strong tidal motion. Using the same principle as river hydroelectric power, the flow of water from ebbing and flowing tides turns the turbines and generates power.

HYDROELECTRIC
Water flowing in a river is channelled through submerged turbines that drive electrical generators. To control the flow of water, the river is often, but not always, dammed.

SOLAR – PHOTOVOLTAIC

Sunlight energy is converted directly into electricity when it hits specially engineered cells made from silicon "doped" with impurities. The cost of manufacturing photovoltaic cells has been very high, but is falling.

SOLAR – THERMAL

The energy carried by sunlight is trapped, concentrated, and used to heat water. This can be used for central heating or, if converted to steam, to drive conventional turbines that generate electricity.

RENEWABLE ENERGY SOURCES

WIND

The power of the turbulent atmosphere is harnessed by wind turbines, which capture energy in the rotation of their aerofoil-shaped blades. This energy is then used to turn electrical generators.

GEOTHERMAL HEAT

The vast reservoir of heat beneath the earth's crust can be tapped, either where it naturally emerges at the surface as geysers and hot springs, or by pumping water or some other fluid below ground to capture the stored heat.

WAVES

Devices that lie on the surface of the sea and move with the rise and fall of passing waves can generate electricity, which is then transmitted through cables laid on the ocean floor.

Leading the way

The business world is starting to see the benefits of using renewable energy sources, and many firms are making it a priority to sign up to renewable energy. In 2008, for example, long-time oilman T. Boone Pickens put together an investment package for a massive wind farm in the US, saying that it was exciting to consider a resource that, unlike his oilfields, would not dry up and need replacing. In the UK, many major firms have signed up to Ecotricity, an energy company that invests in renewable energy power sources, such as wind farms. And in 2006, Bao Steel – the largest iron and steel conglomerate in China – committed itself to buying as much wind-power as possible.

RENEWABLES: HOW THEY STACK UP

TYPE/LEADING COUNTRIES	PROS	CONS
Wind India, US, Germany, Spain, China	A hugely abundant resource that usually becomes more abundant in winter, when energy is needed. Relies on well-proven technologies.	Relatively unpredictable so back-up or storage is needed. Some opposition on the grounds that turbines are considered unsightly and dangerous to wildlife.
Tidal UK, Russia, US, Canada, India	Absolutely reliable and predictable – the size and timing of the tide are known.	The technology is new; tidal power stations may threaten valuable habitats in estuaries.
Waves Portugal, Scotland, England, US	More predictable than wind, but less reliable than tidal.	Wave-power is in development. Devices must be able to resist the most severe storms.
Hydroelectric China, Canada, US, Russia, Brazil, Norway	Extremely reliable, and based on proven technology.	New dam construction inevitably leads to large-scale habitat destruction, and so attracts opposition from environmentalists.
Solar Germany, US, Spain, Japan, India, Australia	The amount of sunlight over a given area is fairly predictable seasonally. The technology is well developed.	Energy in sunlight is diffuse so large installations needed. Photovoltaics that produce electricity are still expensive.
Geothermal Iceland, Mexico, US, Phillipines, Africa	Reliable and weather conditions do not affect supply.	Emits small quanitities of CO_2 although significantly less than the combustion of fossil fuels.

IN FOCUS... A HELPING HAND

Having a government that is informed and positive about the energy form that interests your firm can be very useful. In Germany, the government has taken a proactive role in promoting solar and wind power, putting feed-in tariffs – compulsory higher-priced tariffs for energy generated from renewable sources – in place. As a result, German renewable companies are now world leaders. For example, Conergy – a renewable energy firm set up in 1998 in Hamburg – has grown and grown, and now has offices in the US, Canada, the Far East, India, Brazil, Mexico, Australia, and across Europe. Conergy has created and broken record after record, including for Germany's largest solar park in 2001, the world's largest solar park in 2002, and the largest photovoltaic park in Asia in 2006. Its turnover exceeded one billion euros in 2007, and it employs over 2,000 staff worldwide.

Generating your own power

Ever more businesses are investing in microgeneration – generating their own power by installing solar photovoltaics, small wind turbines, or solar thermal panels (for hot water). Though initial costs may be high, there are numerous long-term benefits: microgeneration helps protect a business from rising energy costs; it provides independence from power outages; it cuts the organization's carbon footprint; and it sends out a clear and visible message to all stakeholders that you are genuinely committed to going green. Internet auction firm eBay, for example, has installed solar panels that it estimates will supply 18 per cent of the power it needs, saving up to $100,000 a year. Before considering microgeneration, you should ensure that your buildings are well insulated and use energy efficiently – these simple measures will give you savings faster, with little investment.

Changing to green fuels

Combustion of fossil fuels to power our vehicles is one of the greatest contributors of man-made CO_2 emissions, and so there has been a great focus on finding sustainable, low-carbon alternatives. A range of green fuel solutions are in development or already in use – these could be an effective way to reduce your carbon footprint, so it pays to keep up with advances.

Developing alternative fuels

Replacing fossil fuels is proving complicated, but research and development into alternative vehicle fuels is gathering pace, and there are already many options out there. However, many of these also have problems, and it is increasingly clear that there is no quick-fix solution to the problem of how to power our vehicles if we want to simultaneously reduce our CO_2 emissions.

Using hydrogen and air power

There are two ways to produce energy from hydrogen: combustion, where hydrogen is burned in the same way as fuel in standard engines; and fuel-cell conversion, where the conversion of hydrogen and oxygen to water produces energy that powers a motor. Hydrogen prototypes exist, but it will be several years before they are affordably on the market. The current method of turning hydrogen into a fuel is too energy intensive and emits more CO_2 per mile than petrol, so work is needed before it can be considered a viable alternative.

Vehicles powered by compressed air have been around for while, but are unlikely candidates for a new portable power supply, chiefly because storing energy as compressed air is less efficient than charging a battery with the same amount of energy.

Using electricity

Electric vehicles are powered by an electric motor that runs on energy stored in a rechargeable battery – a vehicle is literally plugged in to the mains to fill up on fuel. Electric cars were initially not taken seriously, but this changed in 2006 when US car manufacturer Tesla launched the Roadster – an electric high-performance car – and it was a huge hit. Electric delivery vehicles have also taken off, with a number of firms, including a major supermarket chain, moving over part or all of their fleets. However, unless the electricity used in electric vehicles is produced from renewable or nuclear power sources, it is still responsible for CO_2 emissions.

Toyota and Honda have both won huge plaudits for their development of a hybrid engine,

which uses both a petrol or diesel engine plus an electric motor (powered by a rechargeable storage device). This is only a partial solution, however, as the petrol or diesel used will still emit CO_2.

Wal-Mart has embraced the idea of hybrid technology, and is developing the "dual-mode diesel-electric drive-train", which will use "regenerative braking". On braking, the vehicle reverses its electric motor, effectively turning it into a generator that creates electricity to power a motor. This operates in conjunction with a diesel engine.

 IN FOCUS... BIOFUELS

Fuels made from organic materials, such as wheat, palm oil, and oilseed rape, briefly looked as if they would be a viable replacement for fossil fuels, but investors failed to see the inevitable side effects. In 2008, as wealthy countries poured money into biofuels, farmers switched crops, and as a result international food prices soared, leading to a worldwide food crisis. On top of this, biofuels that have been produced from purpose-grown crops actually produce the same carbon emissions as fossil fuels, due to the energy-intensive nature of the farming practices used. Biofuels produced from waste materials, however, are a different matter and may genuinely offer a low-carbon alternative. Cadbury, the UK confectionary producer, for example, has already carried out trials on turning its chocolate waste into biofuels.

Exploring carbon trading

As more and more countries and organizations pledge to meet carbon reduction targets, so carbon trading systems that allow CO_2 emissions to be traded – just like stocks and shares – are growing. Over the next couple of decades, as these systems strengthen, they will begin to exert pressure on all organizations to cut their carbon emissions.

Achieving emissions targets

*Carbon credits — unit amounts of CO_2 emissions that can be bought and sold in carbon trading schemes.

Expressed very simply, carbon trading places a price on CO_2. If you are included in a trading scheme and your CO_2 emissions are higher than the targets you have been set, you will have to pay.

The basic principle behind most carbon markets is Cap and Trade. The regulatory system of the trading scheme sets a cap – a limit – on the amount of CO_2 each participant is allowed to emit. Participants make efforts to reduce their emissions, but are also able to trade with one another in order to remain below that cap. Those that are producing less than their cap will have a surplus of carbon credits*, which they can sell to those that are exceeding theirs.

IN FOCUS... THE CLEAN DEVELOPMENT MECHANISM (CDM)

Under the Kyoto Protocol, it is possible to earn additional carbon credits by financing carbon-reducing projects in other countries – the building of a solar plant in Africa, for example. The CDM has allowed countries some flexibility in the way they work towards their Kyoto targets, and is also potentially a useful way of bringing money from the developed world into the developing world. However, the CDM requires that it is proven that the project would not have been undertaken without this investment (known as the requirement of "additionality"), and in practice this is turning out to be extremely difficult. Corruption is also a concern.

Carbon markets

At present, there are two main carbon markets, plus a number of smaller systems:

- **Kyoto** The Kyoto Protocol requires all developed countries signed up to it to hit targets for reducing CO_2 emissions by 2012. Countries can do this by making changes to reduce emissions; signing up to the Clean Development Mechanism; and also by buying carbon credits (known as Assigned Amount Units or AAUs) from countries that are already meeting their targets.

- **European Emission Trading Scheme** Most EU members have signed to the ETS, a system that assigns targets to certain highly polluting sectors of industry, such as power production. Participants can meet their targets through carbon reduction, and by purchasing carbon credits (which under this scheme are called EU Allowances or EUAs) from organizations that have a surplus of credits.

- **Smaller markets** There are several smaller carbon markets proposed or in existence around the world. For example, in the US, organizations can sign up to the Chicago Climate Exchange – a voluntary carbon trading market, while the state of New South Wales in Australia has its own mandatory carbon market already in place.

IN FOCUS... IS CARBON TRADING THE ANSWER?

Many critics of carbon trading are concerned that it may be the wrong way to approach the problem of our increasing carbon emissions. Economists point out that the systems come with plenty of regulatory muddle, making monitoring problematic. Environmentalists say that these systems just shift reductions from one place to another, and distract from the urgent need to make proper reductions and make them quickly. The first phase of the EU Emission Trading Scheme collapsed because the EU had allocated too many carbon credits, and there has also been criticism of the way in which credits are allocated. These problems obviously need to be ironed out. However, the EU has intimated that in successive phases the cap will be gradually reduced in order to ensure a slow reduction of carbon emissions right across the board. If it really does begin to operate in this way, businesses will be compelled to make genuine reductions, the cost of carbon will increase, and this market will begin to operate in a useful manner.

Offsetting your carbon emissions

Voluntary carbon offsetting is a spin-off from the CDM that briefly looked as if it would be the great hope for businesses planning to go green. The idea that an organization could offset its own emissions by paying someone else to reduce theirs – by, for example, planting trees, collecting the methane gas from animal excreta, or installing renewable power – is obviously appealing. But the flaws in the idea rapidly became clear. Schemes were being mismanaged and mis-sold. Some were offering carbon savings in the future that clearly could not be guaranteed, and were overestimating their current savings. The introduction of certification schemes for carbon offsets have since gone some way to rectifying this situation. More problematic, however, is the public's instinctive distrust of the idea. To some, it seems nonsensical to allow firms to just buy their way out of reducing their footprints – the whole ethos of going green is about reducing your own impact, rather than just paying someone else to do it for you.

If you do choose to use carbon offsetting as a route to reducing your footprint, remember that first you must make every conceivable effort to improve your own emissions – carbon offsets should be a last resort.

Going carbon neutral

The idea of going carbon neutral – reducing your carbon footprint to zero – is extremely fashionable at the moment, but few businesses genuinely attain neutrality. In practical terms, going carbon neutral involves an organization reducing its carbon emissions as much as it possibly can, and then offsetting the reminder. There are, at present, a number of problems with setting and achieving targets of carbon neutrality. Firstly, there is still uncertainty over the accurate calculation of carbon footprints, which makes it difficult to set accurate targets. Furthermore, if businesses use carbon offsetting in order to reach carbon neutrality, the question of whether the offsetting projects have accurately measured the emission reductions they are achieving is raised. With these caveats in mind, current claims of carbon neutrality should be treated with a degree of skepticism. However, it is a worthwhile goal, and if it drives businesses to reduce their carbon emissions, then it will have a postive impact on the environment.

TIP

SET REALISTIC TARGETS
Some businesses are talking about going carbon positive, perhaps by using renewable sources that generate more energy than the organization can use. If you choose to set eyecatching targets such as this, be sure that you can back them up with some radical ways to cut your emissions or you may be accused of greenwash.

✔ CHECKLIST
BUYING CARBON OFFSETS

	YES	NO
• Are you sure that carbon offsetting is compatible with your overall environmental strategy?	☐	☐
• Do you have a definition of what you want from your offsets?	☐	☐
• Have you spoken to a wide variety of offset firms?	☐	☐
• Have you thoroughly researched any potential offset firms to make sure they meet both legal and your own standards?	☐	☐
• Have you checked that any potential offsets you may choose are registered with a standards agency?	☐	☐
• Have you confirmed that your chosen offsets will be compliance-ready should the market alter?	☐	☐

Reporting carbon emissions

As more and more governments begin to place environmental responsibilities on consumers and business, it looks increasingly likely that businesses are going to be required to measure and report on the progress they are making towards reducing their CO_2 emissions.

Accounting for your carbon

It is impossible to contemplate modern business life without standardized financial reporting systems. Imagine if businesses had to operate on best guesses of their financial situation rather than accurate figures, or if each organization was using financial reporting systems of their own devising. Yet this was the case for the auditing of CO_2 emissions in the early 2000s. This situation is now changing with the development of straightforward, standardized systems for carbon reporting. As these systems are implemented, they will start to put requirements on businesses to collect and compile detailed information about their CO_2 emissions and submit this data to an independent party for assessment.

IN FOCUS... WILL CARBON REPORTING BECOME MANDATORY?

Many governments around the world are contemplating the introduction of legislation that makes carbon reporting a legal requirement for all businesses. This is a logical step – countries that have set targets for reducing overall emissions, such as China and the UK, for example, need to measure their emissions in a methodical and standardized way in order to assess whether they are meeting those targets. What makes it more likely is that many businesses are in favour of mandatory carbon reporting, believing that it will standardize reporting systems, and encourage reluctant firms to make steps towards reducing their emissions.

Voluntary reporting

There is an increasing trend for businesses to undertake voluntary reporting. The Carbon Disclosure Project (CDP), for example, which represents investors from around the world, is an independent organization that supplies questionnaires to large businesses asking them to reveal their carbon footprints. Since its inception in 2000, the project has grown and grown, and now lists Rupert Murdoch, Bill Clinton, and Angela Merkel amongst its supporters. The CDP's argument for voluntary reporting is that you can't manage what you can't measure – and that by taking the lead in reporting their emissions, businesses can show leadership in their field.

Compiling reports

The general experience of organizations that are already reporting – to the CDP or elsewhere – is that it is a useful exercise but can also be a fairly time-consuming one that may require staff assigned to it on a full-time basis. As carbon reporting is essentially an extension of carbon footprinting, organizations that are already making these measurements find that they are well prepared to report.

Carbon reporting can clash with the financial reporting year, so integrating both reporting calendars can be extremely useful. By looking at them at the same time, you may also gain interesting insights into these two sides of your business.

GETTING READY TO REPORT

FAST TRACK

OFF TRACK

FAST TRACK	OFF TRACK
"We're measuring our carbon footprint."	"Our company doesn't have a carbon footprint."
"Climate change affects everyone – we all need to take responsibility."	"Climate change won't be a problem for my business."
"We've put a great deal of time and thought into the best way to reduce our environmental impact."	"I don't know if it will affect us – I haven't really thought about it."

Spotting new opportunities

Just as in any other area of business, the environmental challenges the world is facing will also open up opportunities for those that keep an eye to the future. These include the opportunity to take the lead in brand new fields to broaden the outlook of their businesses; and to enter into new conversations and develop closer relationships with their customers.

TIP

CULTIVATE INNOVATIVE THINKING

Make sure there are plenty of chances for new ideas to reach you. Hold regular meetings with your staff and with the green team and encourage them to talk through current issues and future possibilities.

Thinking ahead

Around the world, there are already many examples of businesses that spotted opportunities early and ran with them, and are now reaping the rewards for their forward-thinking approach. Those who invested early in renewables for their own energy production, for example, are now making savings as fuel bills increase year on year. Organizations that cut their journey times and simplified their distribution networks, or that invested in lightweight lorries and packaging, are now saving on fuel costs. And those that invested in renewable power firms are, in some cases, seeing those investments rocket in value. The challenge for today's businesses is to spot the next success stories.

CASE STUDY

Reading the market
The car manufacturer Toyota, founded in Japan in 1937, has been at the forefront of the car market for the past few decades. Its success has been based on scenting out what consumers were going to need, and then providing it. When oil shortages began to bite in the US in the 1970s, for example, Toyota imported smaller, more efficient cars into the country, out-competing the American automobile manufacturers that were still making huge engines. The same thing happened 20 years later: while US car manufacturers were making enormous SUVs, Toyota concentrated on perfecting its hybrid engine. When the price of gasoline began to rise and concerns about climate change moved into the mainstream, it was perfectly placed to respond to the demand for greener vehicles, and in 2008 it was ranked the world's largest automobile company.

Leading your field

Canny businesses are continually on the look-out for opportunities to get ahead of their competition. Areas that are likely to open up in the future include:

- **New products** The future is bright for the inventors of genuinely useful products that have a significantly lower impact on the environment.

- **Clean power production** Big business has come to understand the potential of new forms of power, and is investing heavily in research and development. Those that come up with viable business models for producing green power will be the success stories of tomorrow.

- **Green consultancy** Businesses will increasingly need advice to help tackle the many challenges of going green, and organizations that can assess, audit, and provide expert guidance will find that there is more and more demand for their services.

- **Green specialists** As legal requirements tighten, businesses will increasingly need members of staff in green-specific roles, such as with a remit of monitoring and reporting on green progress, or specializing in education and outreach work. Those that have specialist knowledge and experience will be most in demand and command the highest salaries.

Index

Acknowledgements

Author's acknowledgements

The author would like to thank the staff at Forum for the Future, Greenstone Carbon Management, the Carbon Disclosure Project, Ethical Corporation, and GNL Social and Community Affairs department for their willingness to share their expertise. Thanks also to the many others who allowed me to pick their brains on the best way to green your business. The teams at cobalt id and Dorling Kindersley have been both patient and incisive, and my thanks finally to Mike, Sam, Ben, and Joe.

Publisher's acknowledgements

The publisher would like to thank Neil Mason, Hilary Bird for indexing, and Charles Wills for co-ordinating Americanization.

Picture credits

The publisher would like to thank the following for their kind permission to reproduce their photographs:

1 iStockphoto.com: Ettore Marzocchi; 4–5 iStockphoto.com: Grafissimo; 8–9 iStockphoto.com: Boguslaw Mazur; 12–13 iStockphoto.com: David Marchal; 15 (bottom far left) iStockphoto.com: 7nuit; 15 (bottom left) iStockphoto.com: 7nuit; 15 (bottom right) iStockphoto.com: 7nuit; 15 (bottom far right) iStockphoto.com: 7nuit; 19 iStockphoto.com: Pali Rao; 22 iStockphoto.com: Rebecca Grabill; 26–27 iStockphoto.com: LoopAll; 29 iStockphoto.com: sweetym; 31 Alamy images: PSL Images;

33 iStockphoto.com: gabyjalbert; 34 iStockphoto.com: gabyjalbert; 35 iStockphoto.com: gabyjalbert; 36–7 Corbis: Matthias Kulka/zefa; 39 iStockphoto.com: Russell Tat; 40 (bottom) iStockphoto.com: Edward Grajeda; 40 (centre right) iStockphoto.com: appleuzr; 44–45 iStockphoto.com: Grafissimo; 50–51 iStockphoto.com: Ryan Burk; 56–57 Corbis: Mark A. Johnson; 59 Alamy images: Michael McKee; 60–61 iStockphoto.com: Leon Goedhart; 63 iStockphoto.com: Stephen Strathdee

Every effort has been made to trace the copyright holders. The publisher apologizes for any unintentional omission and would be pleased, in such cases, to place an acknowledgement in future editions of this book.